THE POC[TO THE

C000088975

BALDRIGE AWARD CRITERIA

Mark Graham Brown

Sixth Edition

QUALITY RESOURCES.
A Division of The Kraus Organization Limited
902 Broadway, New York, New York 10010

Quality Resources
A Division of The Kraus Organization Limited
902 Broadway
New York, New York 10010
(212) 979-8600   (800) 247-8519
www.qualityresources.com
E-mail: info@qualityresources.com

ISBN 0-527-76353-5

Printed in the USA 01 00 99   10 9 8 7 6 5 4 3 2 1

Acknowledgments

I would like to thank the following individuals for their suggestions to improve this book: Carol Pletcher, Cargill; Martin Smith, New England Telephone; Ann Wolfe, Air Products and Chemicals; Craig Skrivseth, Appleton Papers. I also wish to thank Jim Springer of Appleton Papers, who gave me the idea for this book, and Lynn Berner-Kilbourn, who did an exceptional job of editing and formatting the book.

MGB

Table of Contents

Introduction

This guide is designed to help you understand the criteria for the Malcolm Baldrige National Quality Award. It is not about the award, or how to win it. Rather, it is about how to interpret and use the criteria to improve your organization.

Most organizations that use the Baldrige criteria have no interest in applying for, or winning, the award. The Baldrige criteria are being used by thousands of organizations around the world to evaluate their progress toward becoming the best in their fields.

This guide is divided into two parts. Part I, a question and answer section, provides the answers to the questions most commonly asked about the award and the criteria. Part II provides a brief explanation of each of the 19 items in the Baldrige criteria and lists the characteristics of organizations that excel in each of these 19 factors.

If the material in this quick reference guide sparks your interest in the Baldrige criteria or the Malcolm Baldrige National Quality Award, you can obtain more information from the sources listed at the end of the book.

Part I: Questions & Answers

Answers to some of the questions frequently asked about the Malcolm Baldrige National Quality Award criteria.

Q: Why is our company using the Baldrige criteria to do assessments?

A: Thousands of organizations, both large and small, use the Baldrige criteria as a guideline for improvement. Most of these organizations have little or no interest in applying for, or winning, the Baldrige Award—their objective is to achieve a better run organization, not a trophy.

More than 1 million copies of the Baldrige criteria have been distributed, yet, in the past few years, less than 50 companies have applied for the award each year. This suggests that most organizations use the criteria to improve performance, rather than to win an award. The real benefits are:

- More satisfied customers.
- Happier employees.
- Increased sales, profits, and market share.
- Long-term survival.

Q: We don't have a quality initiative or program in our organization any more, so why would we even look at the Baldrige criteria?

A: The Baldrige criteria are not about quality or TQM anymore. In 1995, the word "quality" was removed from all parts of the criteria, because it was felt to be limiting, and only one dimension of what makes a healthy organization. Well-run companies are concerned with profits, customers, employees, safety, new product development, and a whole list of aspects besides just quality. The Baldrige Award did start out as a prize for the companies that had the best quality programs. It has evolved into a set of criteria for evaluating the overall health of an organization. Focusing on quality and forgetting about other factors (like financial results) is not a good way to run any organization. The new Baldrige criteria look at how you balance all aspects of performance.

Q: Haven't some of the Baldrige winners gotten into financial trouble?

A: Back in the late 1980s and early 1990s, some Baldrige winners did have financial problems. It's easy to understand why, however. Baldrige did not look at financial results—it looked at quality and customer satisfaction. Early winners often had great quality and customer satisfaction, but later found that this did not translate into improved profits. Since the mid-1990s, Baldrige has put a great deal of emphasis on financial results and all other areas of a company's performance, along with quality.

The 12 years worth of data on Baldrige winners reveals that those companies that are publicly traded outperform the Standard & Poor's (S&P) Index by 3 to 1! The S&P has done very well over the last few years, so the performance of the Baldrige winners is quite impressive. Even companies that are Baldrige finalists outperform the S&P by a 2 to 1 margin. Based on all of these data, it would be foolish for a company to ignore the Baldrige criteria in today's competitive environment. Solectron, the only company to win 2 Baldrige Awards (1991 and 1997), has increased stock value by over 500%

since winning the award in 1991, and has gone from 1800 employees to about 22,000 over that same time period. These data suggest that the Baldrige criteria are the best roadmap toward becoming a more successful company.

Q: How do I apply the Baldrige criteria to assess a facility or department?

A: The criteria are written to assess an entire company or a single business unit. To use the Baldrige criteria to evaluate your facility or department, you need to translate slightly. It is helpful to look at your department or facility as a separate company. Imagine that everyone in your department left the company and formed an organization that sells your services back to the company. From this perspective it is easier to determine who your customers are, and what products/services you provide for them.

In the Baldrige criteria, the word "customer" refers to external customers. Because all of your customers may be inside the company, you need to apply a broader meaning to words like "customer" and "supplier."

Similarly, when assessing areas such as human resources or corporate citizenship, put the item in the context of your department or facility.

Q: What are the seven categories in the Baldrige criteria, and what do they focus on?

A: The seven categories in the Baldrige criteria and their corresponding point values are as follows:

1.0	Leadership	125 points
2.0	Strategic Planning	85 points
3.0	Customer and Market Focus	85 points
4.0	Information and Analysis	85 points
5.0	Human Resource Focus	85 points
6.0	Process Management	85 points
7.0	Business Results	450 points
		TOTAL 1000 points

Fifty-five percent of the points in the Baldrige criteria focus on how the organization is run; the remaining 45% of the points focus on the results achieved. Categories 1.0 through 6.0 (550 points) focus on the company's approaches or systems.

The criteria do not tell you the best method for running your business. Rather, they look for evidence of a systematic approach that is tailored to the needs of your business and culture. Category 7.0, Business Results, asks about your financial, customer, and employee satisfaction performance. All important results in running a business are assessed.

The seven categories of the Baldrige criteria are subdivided into 19 items, which are further subdivided into the 27 areas that must be addressed. The figure below shows how the criteria are organized. This guide explains each of the 19 examination items. The 27 areas to address are not covered in detail.

The Baldrige Criteria

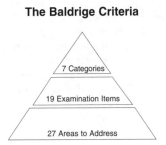

7 Categories

19 Examination Items

27 Areas to Address

Q: How do the seven categories work together as a system?

A: By definition, a system is a series of processes that are followed sequentially to achieve a desired result. Each of the major components of the system has inputs, processes, outputs of results, and ideally, feedback loops. The figure on the inside front cover shows how the Baldrige criteria work as a system.

In the Baldrige criteria as a system, the learning of customers' wants and needs are the inputs (Section 3.1). On the basis of that input, the leadership sets the direction of the company, and defines its mission, values, products and/or services (Category 1.0: Leadership).

Next, the company decides on its overall strategy for success, identifies performance metrics, and sets goals for improvement (Categories 2.0 Strategic Planning and 4.0 Information and Analysis).

Once measures and plans have been developed, the company designs systems and processes for its people (5.0 Human Resource Focus), its customers (3.2 Customer Satisfaction and Relationships), and its major work processes (6.0 Process Management).

All of these systems should produce internal results such as sales, profits, and high-quality products and services, and external results such as customer satisfaction and repeat business or market share (Category 7, Business Results).

Every item in the Baldrige criteria that asks about approaches and the implementation of approaches also asks about built-in feedback loops and continuous improvement.

Q: How are the 1999 Baldrige criteria different from previous years?

A: The Baldrige criteria went through a major rewrite in 1997. Since then only minor changes have been made to the criteria. This year's changes include a few minor additions and deletions from the 1998 version, but nothing major. Some of the specific changes for 1999 are:

- The number of items has been reduced from 20 to 19, and the areas to address have been reduced from 29 to 27. Last year's item 4.2 that asked about comparative/competitor data has been incorporated in 4.1 for 1999.

- All items have been rewritten as questions that should be answered by the applicant, which should improve the clarity of the criteria.

- Titles of the items have been written more concisely and clearly.

- Points for Human Resource Results have increased from 50 to 80, signifying a good balance between needs of shareholders, customers, and employees.

Q: Can you explain how the Baldrige criteria are a roadmap for a better organization?

A: The Baldrige criteria have become the world's most widely accepted model for running an effective business. The criteria cover almost everything that impacts on running a successful organization. The best way to understand this is to list some very basic factors a successful organization must consider, and to identify where these factors are addressed in the Baldrige criteria. Table 1 provides a list of activities successful companies typically perform, along with the Baldrige criteria item that corresponds to the activity.

**Table 1: The Baldrige Criteria—
A Roadmap for Success**

What Successful Organizations Do	Corresponding Baldrige Item
■ Identify and segment customers; define wants and needs.	■ 3.1 Customer and Market Knowledge
■ Establish mission and direction; define key business drivers; develop leadership process to guide organization.	■ 1.1 Organizational Leadership ■ 2.2 Strategy Deployment
■ Develop goals and strategies based on thorough analysis.	■ 2.1 Strategy Development ■ 2.2 Strategy Deployment
■ Identify key performance measures based on company strategy.	■ 3.2 Customer Satisfaction and Relationships ■ 4.1 Measurement of Organizational Performance ■ 4.2 Analysis of Organizational Performance

What Successful Companies Do	Corresponding Baldrige Item
■ Review performance of all key measures, including financial, operational, supplier performance, customer satisfaction, and employee satisfaction.	■ 1.1 Organizational Leadership ■ 7.1 Customer Focused Results ■ 7.2 Financial and Market Results ■ 7.3 Human Resource Results ■ 7.4 Supplier/Partner Results ■ 7.5 Organizational Effectiveness Results
■ Design high quality products/services that meet current and future customer needs.	■ 6.1 Product and Service Processes
■ Design jobs and organizations to promote high performance from employees; train and motivate employees to continuously delight customers.	■ 5.1 Work Systems ■ 5.2 Employee Education, Training, and Development ■ 5.3 Employee Well-Being and Satisfaction

What Successful Companies Do	Corresponding Baldrige Item
■ Define, control, and continuously improve all key processes.	■ 6.1 Product and Service Processes ■ 6.2 Support Processes
■ Work with suppliers and vendors to ensure consistent high quality goods and services.	■ 6.3 Supplier and Partnering Processes
■ Manage customer relationships to maintain high level of satisfaction on an ongoing basis.	■ 3.2 Customer Satisfaction and Relationships
■ Exhibit good corporate citizenship; perform well in areas of public health, environment, ethics.	■ 1.2 Public Responsibility and Citizenship
■ Demonstrate excellent trends and levels in all result areas	■ 7.1 Customer Focused Results ■ 7.2 Financial and Market Results ■ 7.3 Human Resource Results ■ 7.4 Supplier/Partner Results ■ 7.5 Organizational Effectiveness Results

Q: How do the Baldrige criteria apply to a small business?

A: The items in the 1999 criteria are relevant to a small business as well as a big corporation. Small businesses must have good systems and results to keep them in business. The basic difference in your approaches as a small business are levels of formality. A small business does not necessarily need a formal strategic plan or product development and supplier management system. It does need at least an informal approach to all of the elements in the Baldrige criteria, however. For example, you might not need a structured training curriculum for new employees if you only have 25 of them. You might use structured on-the-job training, however, as a way of bringing new hires up to speed. This training can be supplemented with some packaged courses and training materials purchased from outside vendors.

A small business also needs good financial, operational, and customer satisfaction results. Results are more crucial for a small business, because you may not have the reserves to survive a slow period or a loss of a major customer. All of the Baldrige criteria apply to a small business, at least in spirit. Look for ways to meet the Baldrige ideals without adding too much formality to your systems and processes.

Part II: The Baldrige Criteria

A brief explanation of each of the 19 items in the Baldrige criteria and the characteristics of organizations that excel in each of these 19 factors.

1.0 Leadership

Strong leadership is the key to progress on the journey to becoming world class. The first category of the criteria explores how senior executives and managers define the organization's mission and values, and the direction the organization will take in the future. The two items in Category 1.0 ask about the company's leadership system, and how the company's leader drive effective performance (1.1 Organizational Leadership). In addition, this section asks how the company leads in public responsibility and corporate citizenship (1.2 Public Responsibility and Citizenship).

1.0 Leadership

1.1 Organizational Leadership

Describe how senior leaders guide the organization and review organizational performance.

What Does This Mean?

This item identifies the extent to which senior executives are personally involved in establishing the direction of the company and demonstrating the expressed values. Evidence that executives stay close to the operation is considered important. It also asks about the company's system for communicating direction at all levels, and the actions executives take to ensure the organization's continued success. The way the company is organized is also evaluated here. Lean and flexible are what will get you high marks here, rather than a structure that is rigid, bureaucratic, and has many layers.

What Excellent Companies Do

- Build a strong leadership team that is not dependent on any one individual.

- Executives regularly spend time with employees, customers, and other key stakeholders.

- Have a plan to integrate the Baldrige criteria into the daily operation of the business.

- Design organization structures to facilitate high performance on all important measures.

- Continually look for future opportunities to improve/expand company performance.

1.0 Leadership

1.2 Public Responsibility and Citizenship

Describe how your organization addresses its responsibilities to the public and how your organization practices good citizenship.

What Does This Mean?

This item asks for evidence that the company has a systematic approach to improve performance in public health and safety, environmental protection, and corporate citizenship. Companies should have goals for key aspects of performance in these areas, as well as plans to achieve the goals. The organization should be a leader and role model for other organizations.

The company must also show leadership in corporate citizenship by supporting—and encouraging employee involvement in—schools, community groups, professional associations, and charities. Higher marks are given to organizations that are proactive in their approach to corporate citizenship.

What Excellent Companies Do

- Set stretch goals to improve performance in areas of public health and environmental protection.

- Go beyond mandated performance levels in public safety, environmental, and other areas of regulation.

- Allocate significant resources for activities that relate to corporate citizenship and support of educational, community, charity, and professional organizations.

- Allow employees time on the job to support professional and community organizations.

- Link corporate citizenship efforts to marketing plans and company image.

- Become known for supporting one or two causes.

2.0 Strategic Planning

Category 2.0 asks about annual and longer-term planning processes. It is the only section that gives credit for intentions rather than accomplishments. Item 2.1 asks about strategy development and Item 2.2 asks about the company's actual goals and plans, and how they are communicated.

2.1 Strategy Development

Describe your organization's strategy development process to strengthen organizational performance and competitive position. Summarize your key strategic objectives.

What Does This Mean?

This extremely important section asks about how you develop your strategic plan, and what it is. It is important to consider a variety of internal and external factors in developing a good plan, and to do planning in a quick and efficient manner. Even more important than the planning process is the content of the plan itself. Organizations need a clear vision and specific objectives and goals. It's important that objectives are not limited to financial ones. Objectives should cover all areas of performance, including customers/markets, employees, suppliers, and products/services.

What Excellent Organizations Do

- Complete a thorough situation analysis that looks at company strengths, weaknesses, opportunities, and threats.

- Write annual operating and longer-term strategic plans in a 1 to 2 month time period with minimal drafts.

- Focus the planning process on strategic thinking rather than creating a binder.

- Develop a clear vision and identify key success factors, and objectives or goals to become a leader in its industry.

- Link goals to customer requirements, competitor strategies, and assessments of organizational strengths and weaknesses.

2.0 Strategic Planning

2.2 Strategy Deployment

Describe your organization's strategy deployment process. Summarize your organization's action plans and related performance measures. Project the performance of these key measures into the future.

What Does This Mean?

This section looks at how you set specific targets and develop action plans or strategies for achieving the goals asked about in the previous section. Annual and longer-term targets should be specified for each performance measure. In addition, you must present a summary of the major strategies you will use to hit your targets. This item also asks about how you communicate the plan to employees and others, and ensure that all organizational plans are well integrated. Finally, you need to project where you will be in the next 3 to 5 years relative to competitors if you hit all of your targets.

What Excellent Organizations Do

- Identify key success factors that differentiate your organization from key competitors.

- Set measurable targets for each measure of performance, based upon relevant data (e.g., competitors, resources, customer needs, etc.).

- Define specific strategies or action plans for hitting targets.

- Communicate plans to all levels of employees and partners so they understand their role in helping the organization achieve its vision.

- Adapt or change targets and strategies quickly as the business environment changes.

- Predict how achievement of targets will change the organization's position in the marketplace over the next 2 to 5 years.

3.0 Customer and Market Focus

This category asks how you identify customers and their requirements and manage relationships that keep them satisfied. Item 3.1 asks how you identify customers and define their needs. Item 3.2 asks how you win and keep customers and addresses customer satisfaction measures.

3.1 Customer and Market Knowledge

Describe how the company determines short- and longer-term requirements, expectations, and preferences of customers to ensure the relevance of current products/services and to develop new opportunities.

What Does This Mean?

If you were to write an application for the Baldrige Award, this might be the section to start with because it defines what the organization does. This section asks, "Who are your customers and what do they want from your products/services?" You need to list the markets or industries you currently sell to, and explain how you determine each customer type's wants and expectations. It is important not only to use several methods to identify customer requirements, but to use them often. Customers' wants and expectations change frequently.

This section also asks about future customers, and what their requirements will be. These are tough questions to answer; however, the most successful companies today look at industry trends and predict how they will impact their products/services. Successful companies also look beyond current customers and identify new industries or types of customers.

As with all Baldrige items that ask about approaches, it is important to show a trend of continuously evaluating and improving methods of identifying customer requirements.

What Excellent Companies Do

- Clearly identify customers and segment them by market, geography, or other categories.

- Use a variety of methods to identify customer requirements and priorities.

- Continuously evaluate and improve methods to determine customer requirements.

- Conduct research to identify potential future customers and their needs.

- Identify the requirements of noncustomers or customers of competitors.

3.0 Customer and Market Focus

3.2 Customer Satisfaction and Relationships

Describe how the company determines the satisfaction of its customers and builds relationships, to retain current business and develop new opportunities.

What Does This Mean?

This item asks how you keep customers happy once you have won their business. Most organizations spend more money to gain customers than they do to retain customers. This section asks for evidence of a proactive approach to keeping customers satisfied on an ongoing basis.

Another dimension of keeping customers satisfied is providing an easy outlet for their complaints, and for seeking information. Have a system for tracking all complaints and promptly resolve complaints when they occur. When customers complain, it is an opportunity to win back their trust and good will.

Item 3.1 asked how you learn about customer requirements. This item refers to how you measure what customers think of your products/services after they are purchased. You should also explain how you measure customer satisfaction in item 4.1. This section provides an opportunity to go into more detail.

You should have hard and soft measures of customer satisfaction. Hard measures are measures of customers' actual buying behavior. Soft measures are opinions, gathered through surveys, interviews, and focus groups.

Along with a good mix of hard and soft customer satisfaction data, it is much better to tailor measurements to the markets or types of customers you sell to, rather than use a generic customer satisfaction survey for everyone. Finally, it is important to describe how you build loyalty from important customers, taking into account that customer needs/priorities vary.

3.0 Customer and Market Focus

3.2 Customer Satisfaction and Relationships (continued)

What Excellent Companies Do

- Hire the best and brightest customer contact people, pay them well, thoroughly train them, and give them the authority to solve customer problems without checking with management.

- Define measurable service standards and measure performance against them.

- Provide toll-free help lines or conveniences to make it easy to get information.

- Track all complaints, no matter how minor, and quickly resolve complaints.

- Accumulate information on customers in a central database so that this intelligence can be used to drive improvement.

- Collect a good mix of hard and soft measures of customer satisfaction.

- Define customer satisfaction levels compared to key competitors and industry averages.

- Focus on measuring value and loyalty as well as customer satisfaction.

- Employ a systematic approach to building loyalty from the most valued customers.

4.0 Information and Analysis

Category 4.0 is the foundation of the seven criteria. It addresses how success is measured and data are used to make business decisions. Item 4.1 asks how measurements are determined, and how the database has been improved. Item 4.2 asks about information gathered on competitors and world-class companies that are not necessarily competitors. Item 4.3 asks how data are summarized, analyzed, and used for decision making.

4.1 Measurement of Organizational Performance

Describe how your organization provides effective performance measurement systems for understanding, aligning, and improving performance at all levels and in all parts of your organization.

What Does This Mean?

This item asks if you're measuring the right things and keeping a balanced scorecard. Measures must relate to your key business drivers and success factors and relate to your vision and values. These criteria should select the "vital few" of the many variables that could be measured. It is important that you have a well-balanced set of measures. Your database should include short-term measures such as operational and financial metrics, as well as longer-term measures such as customer satisfaction, market growth, and employee satisfaction. You must continuously refine your measures.

This is one of the most important items in the Baldrige criteria. If you select the wrong things to measure, this will impact your scores in all of the result areas, which amount to almost 50% of the points. This section also asks about data on competitors and other organizations against which you might compare.

What Excellent Companies Do

- Use key business strategies and their vision to select performance measures on their scorecard.

- Keep the number of measurement indices that managers regularly review to no more than 20.

- Include a balance of measures that focuses on the past, present, and future and that relates to the needs of shareholders/owners, customers, and employees.

- Have roughly the same number of measures and data in each section of the company's overall scorecard of metrics.

- Collect a wide variety of data on key competitors.

- Collect data on other non-competitor organizations to use in goal setting and process improvement.

4.0 Information and Analysis

4.2 Analysis of Organizational Performance

Describe how your organization analyzes performance data and information to assess and understand overall organizational performance.

What Does This Mean?

Most organizations collect a great deal of data, but business decisions are often based on instinct and experience. This item looks for evidence that data are used to make business decisions, and explores how various types of data are summarized.

The criteria asks how individual indices are summarized into single measures or ratios. For example, several measures might be summarized into an index. This item also asks if data on customer satisfaction, operational performance, and financial factors are considered together to make business decisions. For example, improving customer satisfaction or product/service quality often costs money. The impact improvements could have on other areas should be analyzed to ensure they warrant the investment.

The Baldrige criteria explain that this is the "central intelligence item" in the entire system. A poor job of summarizing and analyzing data will impact your scores in the sections that deal with areas of planning, process management, and results.

What Excellent Companies Do

- Hold regular meeting at all levels to analyze performance data.

- Summarize individual metrics into aggregate indices or ratios where appropriate, such as a Customer Satisfaction Index (CSI).

- Prioritize performance measures on the basis of strategy and key success factors.

- Conduct research to establish correlation among leading and lagging metrics on the company scorecard.

- Spend as much time focusing on measures that lead to future successes as on metrics that relate to past and present performance.

- Actually use data/facts to make business decisions.

- Show how changes in quality/customer satisfaction impact financial performance.

- Continually improve data analysis processes.

5.0 Human Resource Focus

Category 5.0 addresses the approaches you use with employees to achieve consistently effective performance. The three items address work systems (5.1), training and employee development (5.2), and employee well-being and morale (5.3).

5.1 Work Systems

Describe your organization's work and job design, compensation, career progression, and related workforce practices that enable employees to achieve high performance in your operations.

What Does This Mean?

This section asks how you have designed your organization's structure and jobs to facilitate flexibility, speed, and the delight of customers. How you go about recruiting and selecting the best people for your organization is an important process asked about in this section. The criteria are asking about fundamental changes in the way work is done by employees. Jobs and structures must promote efficiency, flexibility, and satisfaction of employees. The key is to have a human performance system that drives the right behavior.

Approaches to compensate and recognize employees for high performance are also asked about in this section. Financial and nonfinancial rewards should be available to all individuals and teams of employees based upon achievement of high levels of performance. Employee-of-the-month, an annual 4% raise, or other typical approaches will not score high in this section. The criteria are asking for evidence that all employees are treated like business partners and that creativity and effort are incorporated into employee recognition methods.

What Excellent Companies Do

- Design job and organization structures to promote empowerment, efficiency, employee development, and elimination of nonvalue-added efforts.

- Empower employees and teams to implement suggestions rather than relying on suggestion systems.

- Eliminate functional departments and layers of management where possible.

- Employ many recognition programs tailored to individual and group preferences and refine them.

- Compensation systems are set up to reward good performance and drive the right behavior.

5.0 Human Resource Focus

5.2 Employee Education, Training, and Development

Describe how your organization's education and training support the achievement of your business objectives, build employee knowledge, skills, and capabilities, and contribute to improved employee performance.

What Does This Mean?

This item addresses all types of employee training and development: orientation, leadership, safety, performance improvement, technical skills training. It is important that you show evidence of a systematic needs analyses that determines who needs which training when, as well as planned follow-up to ensure the skills learned in the classroom are used on the job. It is not enough to provide employees with training. It is more important to tailor training to individual needs, and collect data to prove the training is effective. Effectiveness is determined by measuring learning and the extent job performance measures improve after training. Information on improvement in both the amount and effectiveness of training should also be included.

What Excellent Companies Do

- Invest up to 5% of payroll costs on training each year.

- Perform systematic needs analyses to determine training needs for all employees.

- Develop curriculums for all key functions/positions.

- Match training media and delivery methods to content and audience characteristics.

- Deliver training in a just-in-time fashion and plan follow-up activities to ensure skills learned in training are used on the job.

- Evaluate training based on trainee reaction, learning, behavior change, and job performance improvement.

- Continually improve training on the basis of feedback.

5.0 Human Resource Focus

5.3 Employee Well-Being and Satisfaction

Describe how your organization maintains a work environment and an employee support work climate that contribute to the well-being, satisfaction, and motivation of all employees.

What Does This Mean?

Leading companies today believe employees must be delighted with the organization before they will go out of their way to delight customers. Many factors—safety, pay, benefits, job design, work environment, workload—contribute to employee satisfaction. This item asks how your organization ensures employees are healthy and happy with their work. It is important to do more than the basics.

This section also asks how employee satisfaction is measured. Employee satisfaction results are reported in Item 7.3. You should have both hard measures of employee satisfaction such as turnover, grievances, and absenteeism, and soft measures such as employee morale or climate surveys. In addition, this section asks for evidence that you have a systematic prevention-based approach to safety and employee health.

What Excellent Companies Do

- Focus on delighting employees rather than simply satisfying them.

- Establish goals for safety and employee satisfaction based on world-class companies.

- Implement a prevention-based approach to safety and employee health.

- Offer pay, benefits, and special services that are better than others in the industry and geographic area.

- Frequently collect data on a wide variety of measures of employee satisfaction.

- Communicate that personal/family lives are more important or just as important as work.

- Establish systems for building and maintaining a loyal and diverse work force.

6.0 Process Management

Category 6.0 defines how key processes are managed and controlled. Item 6.1 asks how new products/services are designed, and how work processes are managed and improved. 6.2 asks for similar information for support areas such as finance or purchasing. 6.3 asks how suppliers and partners are managed.

6.1 Product and Service Processes

Describe how your organization manages key product and service design and delivery processes.

What Does This Mean?

This item requires a systematic approach to the design of new products or services that is driven by customer needs, and involves all appropriate functions. Evidence should show how your product/service design process is systematic and timely.

Product and service design is not just the responsibility of research and engineering. Every function has products and services (e.g., a new financial report or performance appraisal system) that should be based on customer requirements.

This section also asks you to identify and measure key processes. You will explain your standards and how you keep process performance within acceptable limits. In identifying key processes, list the five to eight major activities you perform in your plant, or in the service delivery portion of your business. A matrix that lists key processes, measures, standards, and control strategies will help you respond to this item.

Evaluate processes to identify opportunities for improvement. Improvement ideas might come from research, benchmarking, new technologies, or customers. This section also asks which key processes have been improved and how extensive the changes or improvements have been.

What Excellent Companies Do

- Design new products and services on the basis of current and projected future customer requirements and priorities.

- Involve a wide variety of disciplines or departments in the design process.

- Define key processes and process measures on the basis of customer requirements.

- Define and implement strategies to keep each process measure in control.

- Use a variety of sources of information to proactively look for ways of improving processes.

- Link process improvement initiatives to strategic plans.

6.0 Process Management

6.2 Support Processes

Describe how your organization manages its key support processes.

What Does This Mean?

This section requires the same information as the previous section, however, it is relative to support processes. If an entire company is being evaluated, this section would include all support functions such as finance, purchasing, engineering, human resources, information systems, sales/marketing, R&D facilities, and legal. For each support area, key processes, measures, standards, and control strategies would be defined. In the case of an individual facility or plant, this section would examine the administrative or support processes. If the scope of the evaluation is a department, this section would ask about administrative functions or processes.

As in section 6.1, this section asks about how opportunities to improve processes are initiated and how key processes have been improved. For example, perhaps you have completely changed the way the company purchases or has implemented a new approach to performance appraisal. Comparisons to other companies should be used to initiate process improvement ideas.

What Excellent Companies Do

- Identify the most important support processes on the basis of the needs and requirements of both internal and external customers.

- Identify and collect data on key measures for each of the major support processes.

- Define standards or control limits for each process measure.

- Use a systematic proactive process to identify process improvement opportunities in support areas.

- Measure levels of internal customer satisfaction for each major support function.

- Continuously improve key support processes.

6.0 Process Management

6.3 Supplier and Partnering Processes

Describe how your organization manages its key supplier and/or partnering interactions and processes.

What Does This Mean?

This section asks for evidence that the organization helps suppliers and partners with their performance. The first step is to explicitly define your requirements. Make sure suppliers know exactly what you want and expect of them. Many companies include suppliers in training programs. Many also certify suppliers. It is important to work with suppliers to help them improve, rather than simply demanding that they meet your standards for quality and price or you will find someone else who will.

Selecting suppliers on price, and always getting competitive bids, is not the approach this section looks for. Rather, the trends in companies that do well on this item are: narrowing the number of suppliers to a few key companies with proven records of exceptional quality at fair prices and trusting suppliers more.

What Excellent Companies Do

- Thoroughly define requirements for all suppliers/ partners and regularly measure how well they meet requirements.

- Reduce the overall number of suppliers to companies with proven track records.

- Cease reliance on inspection of incoming supplier materials and rely more on suppliers to inspect their own products.

- Require suppliers/partners to implement the basics of the Baldrige criteria and help them by providing training and coaching.

- Establish long-term partnering relationships with key suppliers/partners who have proven they can meet or exceed your requirements.

7.0 Business Results

Category 7.0 is the most important of the seven categories and is worth almost half the total points in the Baldrige assessment. All the important results a company tracks are reported here. There are five items in this category — Item 7.1 asks for customer satisfaction results; Item 7.2 asks for financial and market results; Item 7.3 asks for human resource results; Item 7.4 asks for supplier/partner performance results; and Item 7.5 asks for organizational effectiveness results. In each item, examiners look for improvement trends and exceptional levels of current performance, compared to competitors and benchmarks.

7.1 Customer Focused Results

Summarize your organization's customer-focused results, including customer satisfaction and product and service performance results. Segment your results by customer group and market segments, as appropriate. Include appropriate comparative data.

What Does This Mean?

This section asks for graphs of customer satisfaction performance over the past few years. The more years that can be included, the better. As with the other items that ask for results, there are three dimensions of evaluation: levels, trends, and variability.

Data on how customer satisfaction levels compare to those of competitors are also asked for in this item.

Data on soft measures of customer satisfaction from surveys or focus groups should be presented with data on hard measures of buying behavior (e.g., repeat/lost customers, or returns), or internal product service quality measures. Measures of dissatisfaction should also be presented. To evaluate trends, all graphs should include relevant comparative data and benchmarks.

Results in Excellent Companies

- Customer satisfaction data are segmented by market or customer type as appropriate, and all graphs show excellent improvement trends.
- No graphs of customer focused results show flat or declining performance, and any dips in performance are satisfactorily explained.
- All major indicators of customer dissatisfaction show declines over the past five or more years, as well as overall excellent levels of performance.
- Trends over the past three or more years show continuous improvement in hard measures of customer satisfaction, and internal quality measures.
- Levels of performance on hard measures of customer satisfaction show the best performance in the industry on almost all graphs, and benchmark or world-class levels of performance on several graphs.

7.0 Business Results

7.2 Financial and Market Results

Summarize your organization's key financial and marketplace performance results, segmented by market segments, as appropriate. Include appropriate comparative data.

What Does This Mean?

This section asks for two types of results or data: market and financial results. Market results might include gains and losses of customers or market share within certain markets. Financial results are the typical financial measures companies collect data on such as sales, profits, and return on investment. All of the key market and financial measures should be identified in item 4.1. You should have graphs of results on each of these measures for the last five years or more. As with the previous item, results in this area are evaluated by looking at levels, trends, and variability.

Results in Excellent Companies

- Key financial and market results for five or more years show a trend of progressive improvement.

- Profits show a level of performance that is at or above the best companies in the industry.

- The company has clear cause-effect data that show that investments in improvement initiatives have paid off on the bottom line.

- Market and financial measures show benchmark levels of performance, or at least a continuous improving trend, over five or more years.

- No graphs of market or financial indicators show performance to be flat or getting worse over the past few years.

- Dips in performance have been thoroughly analyzed and the factors causing these drops in performance have been corrected.

7.0 Business Results

7.3 Human Resource Results

Summarize your organization's human resource results, including employee well-being, satisfaction, development, and work system performance. Segment your results by types and categories of employees as appropriate. Include appropriate comparative data.

What Does This Mean?

This new section asks for levels and trends in key human resource measures such as safety, turnover, employee morale, and absenteeism. Other measures identified in section 5.0 might also have results presented here. For example, training effectiveness measures, or percentage of employee suggestions implemented. Other statistics might also be presented regarding measures such as recognition of employees or compensation.

Comparative data on how human resource performance compares with competitors, industry averages, and benchmarks should also be presented, to aid in evaluating levels of performance.

Results in Excellent Companies

- Safety results show that impressive improvement trends and/or levels of performance are superior to industry averages and competitors.

- Measures of employee satisfaction indicate that the company "delights" its employees.

- Hard measures of employee satisfaction such as absenteeism and voluntary turnover show improving trends and levels above those of competitors.

- No human resource performance measures show declining trends or levels that are inferior to industry averages or major competitors.

- Results are presented for all key human resource measures identified in section 5.0.

7.0 Business Results

7.4 Supplier and Partner Results

Summarize the results of the organization's supplier and partner performance results. Include appropriate comparative data.

What Does This Mean?

In item 4.1 and 6.3, you identified how supplier/partner performance is measured. Most companies use a mix of hard data and soft data to measure supplier performance. Hard data could be returns of defective merchandise, percentage of defective parts/materials, or delivery dates missed. Soft measures could be ratings of responsiveness or courtesy. Both types of data should be presented from the past few years for your major suppliers.

Most organizations have a great many suppliers, but spend 75% to 80% of their money with a handful of suppliers. These are the suppliers you should have performance data on. If you do not have data on minor suppliers, it will not be held against you. Distributors and other partners are also considered suppliers, so make sure you include data on performance of "upstream" and "downstream" suppliers and partners.

Results in Excellent Companies

- Strong improvement trends in the performance of the company's major suppliers an partners are evident over the past few years.

- Suppliers' levels of performance compare favorably to those of competitors' and benchmark organizations' suppliers.

- The company has shown a reduction over the past few years in the overall number of suppliers it buys goods and services from.

- Data are presented for most major suppliers—those the company spends the most money with.

7.0 Business Results

7.5 Organizational Effectiveness Results

Summarize your organization's key operational performance results that contribute to the achievement of organizational effectiveness. Include appropriate comparative data.

What Does This Mean?

This section asks for any results that may not be included in previous sections. This is a catch-all item that allows you the clause to present performance measures that may be unique to your business or industry. Results presented here might include: internal product/service quality, productivity, innovation, environmental, cycle time, regulatory measures, or performance of new products/services. As with other sections, it is important to present data on competitors, industry averages, and other comparative data.

Results in Excellent Companies

- Results are presented for all key performance measures for which results are not presented earlier.

- Productivity and cycle time both show impressive levels and improvement trends.

- Data on important process measures show improvements and high levels.

- Most graphs should show company performance to be better than all or most key competitors.

- No data are missing on important measures of operational performance.

For Additional Reading

Brown, Mark Graham. *Baldrige Award Winning Quality,* 9th Edition. New York: Quality Resources, 1999.

Brown, Mark Graham. *The Small Business Pocket Guide to the Baldrige Award Criteria.* New York: Quality Resources, 1997.

Garvin, David. "How the Baldrige Award Really Works," *Harvard Business Review,* November/December, 1991, p.80-95.

Hart, Christopher W.L. and Christopher Bogan. *The Baldrige: What It Is, How It's Won, How to Use It to Improve Quality in Your Company,* New York, NY: McGraw-Hill Inc., 1992.

National Institute of Standards and Technology. Malcolm Baldrige National Quality Award, 1996 Award Criteria. Gaithersberg, MD: NIST, 1996.